To:

*From the fullness of his grace
we have all received one blessing after another.*

JOHN 1:16

From:

The heartfelt prayers at the conclusion of each meditation were written by Kathie Lee's brother, David Epstein, Senior Pastor of Calvary Baptist Church in New York City.

Requests for information should be addressed to:
Inspirio, the gift group of Zondervan
Grand Rapids, Michigan 49530
www.inspirio.com

Associate Publisher: Tom Dean
Project Editor: Rebecca Currington in association with Snapdragon Editorial Group, Inc.
Design Manager: Val Buick
Design: UDG│DesignWorks—Cover, Christopher Gilbert; Interior, Christopher Gilbert/Robin Black

REFLECTIONS AND SCRIPTURES *on* GOD'S GENTLE GRACE

Kathie Lee Gifford

Gentle
Grace

ACKNOWLEDGMENTS

I am "eternally" grateful to the following people for making this project a reality: Linda Klosterman for bringing me to Inspirio. To Tom Dean and his team at Inspirio and Rebecca Currington and Snapdragon Editorial Group for receiving me so graciously. To my dear friend, Christine Gardner, who never loses patience with me even though she deserves to on a daily basis. And to my precious brother, Dave, who always makes such good spiritual sense. Many thanks to my loving family and friends. If I have anything to share at all, it's because I have been so loved.

All of the author's proceeds from the sales of this book will go to Cassidy's Place and the Variety Cody Gifford House, both are a part of the Association to Benefit Children, a national children's advocacy program located in New York City. For more information go to www.a-b-c.org.

*I gratefully dedicate this small, simple book to
my precious Daddy, "Eppie," who went home to heaven
on November 19, 2002.*

*No one ever taught me more about how to live a godly
life, and I miss him every moment of every day. I took a
picture of his hand in my hand right before he died so that
I would always remember how it felt to have a father who
believed in me and guided me and cared for me so much.*

*My earthly father reminds me of my heavenly Father,
and any tear I shed today is a tear of joy because
I have been so rich in their love.*

TABLE OF CONTENTS

WE CAN DEPEND
on His Word

WE CAN DEPEND ON HIS WORD

Kathie Lee Gifford, Phil Sillas

The sky's growing darker
As the evening draws near
The storm clouds have gathered
And the shadows are gone
When all hope has faded
Replaced now with fear
Tell me what can we depend on

We can depend on his word
When all hope is gone
We can still depend on
We can depend on his word

When troubles grow deeper
And the desert is dry
And our hearts are so broken
That we can't even cry
When our faith is wounded
And our joy is gone
Tell me what can we depend on

When the rain comes and the pain comes
And we know that it will
We can still trust
He is still just the same
He still calls us by name

Is There Anything
God Can't Do?

During our together time, my children asked, "Mommy, is there anything God *can't* do? I had to think for a moment.

"Yes," I told them, "He can't break his promises."

"What does that mean?" they responded. I had to pause again.

"Well …," I said, "that means we can absolutely count on him to keep his promises to us. What he says, he will do."

That was all my children needed to hear. They smiled up at me, nodded their heads enthusiastically, and went off to play. *If only my faith were as simple as theirs,* I thought. Then I began to consider the ramifications of what I had just told them.

If God cannot break his promises, then we know that we can stake our lives and our afterlives on them. It's the greatest "insurance" policy ever. So when I say "We can depend on his word," I'm actually saying I can depend on the God of all Creation to do what he says he's going to do. To do otherwise would be to violate his own person. His promises are guaranteed by the same power that keeps the sun in its place and the planets spinning in their orbits.

I hope you'll take hold of that truth and make it part of your life so that when the skies grow dark around you and the winds of discouragement and despair begin to blow, you will not be shaken. His peace will surround you in the midst of the storm.

Believe me, I know how important that can be. I've been through some very private challenges in a very public way. I often cried and questioned God's purpose and wanted to give up. But I didn't!

How did I manage to smile through my tears?

I remembered that my God—the God of all the universe—lovingly created me. He knows all about me and understands every emotion I feel. I know that he will never leave me, that he will accomplish all he has planned for my life, that nothing can separate me from his love. How do I know? He promised!

God has said,

"Never will I leave you;

never will I forsake you."

HEBREWS 13:5

"I know the plans I have for you," declares the LORD, "plans to prosper you and not to harm you, plans to give you hope and a future."

JEREMIAH 29:11

I am convinced that neither death nor life, neither angels nor demons, neither the present nor the future, nor any powers, neither height nor depth, nor anything else in all creation, will be able to separate us from the love of God that is in Christ Jesus our Lord.

ROMANS 8:38–39

You know with all your heart and soul that not one of all
the good promises the LORD your God gave you has failed. Every promise
has been fulfilled; not one has failed.

JOSHUA 23:14

The Lord is faithful to all his promises
and loving toward all he has made.

PSALM 145:13

No matter how many promises God has made, they are "Yes" in Christ.
And so through him the "Amen" is spoken by us to the glory of God.

2 CORINTHIANS 1:20

Heavenly Father,

Thanks for keeping your promises to me. You are truly a God of your word. May my trust in you grow like the faith of a child resting in a parent's love. My hope and trust are well placed in you. Amen.

EVERY DAY
of My Life

It has been twenty-five years since I recorded my last inspirational album. In many ways, I'm the same person I was back then. But in other ways, I'm very different.

I've loved a lot, and I've been hurt a lot. I've succeeded beyond my dreams, and yet, many of my dreams remain unrealized. I still have my mother, but my beloved daddy is gone now. I've made some good choices and some that I regret.

Through the years, however, there has been one powerful constant. God has had a purpose for every triumph and every tear. He leaves no crumbs on his table—he uses absolutely everything for the building of his kingdom in my life.

God doesn't blink! He doesn't sleep. He sees it all, and he cares deeply about every aspect of my life. This single belief has been the guiding, abiding truth in every day I have lived. God is bigger than any mistake I could possible make. He's so big that he can actually use my mistakes to make *me* bigger too.

I love serving such a magnificent God. I take enormous delight in knowing him, loving him, and sharing him. I am so humbled to think that he knows my name. He knows how many hairs are still on my head. He is the architect of every dream I've ever dreamed. He is my dearest, most faithful friend. He is the lover of my soul.

I want every day of my life to be a day when I know I have lived each moment for him. I have tried to be faithful to his call. I have relied on him in my weakness. I have trusted him in my distress. I have thanked him for every sunrise and praised him for every sunset. And,

"When my life is over, and the battle is done
I have His assurance that the battle was won
And life everlasting is waiting for me
He's made a pathway through the clouds
Thru the storm, through the darkness,

Thru the desert, through the sea
He's made a pathway thru the clouds
To all eternity
For you
And me."

I know whom I have believed, and am convinced

that he is able to guard what I have entrusted to him for that day.

2   TIMOTHY   1 : 12

Remember, O LORD, your great mercy and love,

for they are from of old.

Remember not the sins of my youth

and my rebellious ways;

according to your love remember me,

for you are good, O LORD.

PSALM   25 : 6 – 7

Blessed are those who have learned to acclaim you,

who walk in the light of your presence, O LORD.

PSALM   89 : 15

Where can I go from your Spirit?

    Where can I flee from your presence?

If I go up to the heavens, you are there;

    if I make my bed in the depths, you are there.

If I rise on the wings of the dawn

    if I settle on the far side of the sea,

even there your hand will guide me,

    your right hand will hold me fast.

PSALM 139:7–10

This, then is how we know that we belong to the truth, and how

we set our hearts at rest in his presence whenever our hearts condemn us.

For God is greater than our hearts, and he knows everything.

1 JOHN 3:19–20

In Christ we were also chosen, having been predestined according
to the plan of God who works out everything in conformity
with the purpose of his will, in order that we, who were the first to hope
in Christ, might be for the praise of his glory.

EPHESIANS 1:11–12

God,

It must feel awesome to be you—sovereign, eternal, and unchanging. Jesus Christ, the same yesterday, today and forever. But for me, yesterday's gone— it's history. And tomorrow's a mystery. So thank you for today, it's a gift—the present. Reveal your destiny in my life today; fulfill your purpose in every detail. Cause all things—beautiful things, ugly things— to work together for good in my life, because I love you. I know you won't waste anything, Lord—not the glory, and not the pain. Amen

I BELIEVE
in You

I Believe in You

Kathie Lee Gifford, Phil Sillas

Some people believe in happenstance
believe life is random, a matter of chance
Talk it up to coincidence
Chalk it up to experience

Some people believe that there's no grand plan
You can only do the best you can
Cross your fingers, knock on wood
Hope for the best
Wish for the good
That is all you can really do
I don't believe it's really true
'Cause I believe in You

I believe that all things work together for the good
That everything works out the way God always planned it would
And I believe His promises are real
No matter how I feel
I believe His promises are true no matter what I'm going through
'Cause I believe in You

Some people believe in philosophy
Believe there's no need for apology
Or put their faith in the stars above
Accept deception disguised as love

Some people believe life's a tragedy
You're born into a world with no guarantee
And no gift you're given is really free
But I disagree

MY GOD *Lives!*

Some years ago, the renowned astronomer Carl Sagan appeared as a guest on "LIVE." As an avowed atheist, he was explaining in scientific terms that it is impossible for God to exist. As the co-host of the show, I waited until he finished and then remarked that he could set indisputable evidence right in front of a person of faith and it would not change their mind. Surprisingly, he agreed. He had met many such people.

Since that time, I have learned that there is much evidence to support God's existence. But regardless of how much is amassed, it can never be proven beyond a shadow of a doubt—and I believe that's as God intended. He wants us to reach out to him in faith—to touch him with heart power rather than head power.

You see, my belief in God is not a result of scientific verification; nor is it based on a whim, and it's not because I *want* him to exist. I believe in God, first and foremost, because I have spent almost 40 years getting to know him. He is just as real to me, in some ways even more real, than my husband, my children, my friends.

I was amused years ago by a cartoon I saw of a graffiti sign on a subway wall. It read:

"God is dead." *Nietzche*

"Neitzche is dead." *God*

Can I prove he exists? Not scientifically. But I can prove it by the way he has taught me to live: loving when my heart wants to hate, forgiving when I feel justified in holding a grudge, praying for the very people who strike out at me or my loved ones. In other words, my proof is that I do what my nature tells me is impossible. And that's all the evidence I require.

Yes, I believe in Him. And you can too! Reach out by faith, and you will find—just as I did—he lives!

Without faith, it is impossible to please God,
because anyone who comes to him must believe that he exists and
that he rewards those who earnestly seek him.

HEBREWS 11:6

Jesus said, "Because you have seen me, you have
believed; blessed are those who have not seen and yet have believed."

JOHN 20:29

Faith is being sure of what we hope for
and certain of what we do not see.

HEBREWS 11:1

Though you have not seen Christ, you love him;
and even though you do not see him now, you believe in him and
are filled with an inexpressible and glorious joy.

1 PETER 1:8

This is a trustworthy saying that deserves full acceptance (and for this we labor and strive), that we have put our hope in the living God, who is the Savior of all men, and especially of those who believe.

1 TIMOTHY 4:9–10

Jesus said, "Everything is possible for him who believes."

MARK 9:23

O Lord,

I believe in you, but this world is not an easy place to trust you. Grant me a greater sense of your presence; a greater confidence in your word; a greater obedience to your will. And Lord, increase my faith! When I can't trace your hand, help me trust your heart. Amen.

FORGIVE
My Unbelief

There have been times in my life when I wanted to give up. I couldn't see God's hand in my circumstances and my disappointments and hurts seemed to outnumber my blessings. Even though I was surrounded by people, I felt alone. At times like that, I'm reminded that faith is something I am supposed to *do,* even when I don't *feel* like it. Faith is an act of my will.

When I find myself caught up in the emotion of my circumstances, I begin by going to the Lord with three simple words: "Please forgive me." I need his forgiveness for my unbelief, for my lack of faith, for my impatience.

I am not a patient person by nature. In fact, I'm the complete opposite. It is difficult for me to wait for anything. I'm the one that always wants something sent "Federal Express, overnight delivery." Better yet— "Messenger it!"

Isaiah 40:31 says, "Those who wait for the LORD shall renew their strength" (NRSV). But how do I wait? How do I trust the light in the midst of the darkness? It's so simple it's easy to miss. We *ask*. "Ask and it will be given to you," is what we're told in Matthew 7:7. God already knows what we need, whatever it is—he is waiting for us to ask for it.

Every inadequacy in our lives is there for a purpose, too, just as our gifts are. They exist to draw us closer to our Creator. If we were perfect we wouldn't need him! We go to a doctor when we're sick because we believe he will be able to help us. So we must go to the Lord for whatever we need, *believing* that he will help us. He has to, because he has promised to, and he can't break his promises. Whatever storm we are in the midst of, God is not only aware of it—he's in control of it!

Asking for forgiveness allows me to capsize guilt and shame and re-establish myself in relation to God and his precious promises. This act puts things in perspective for me and changes my focus from myself to God, from my faithlessness to his faithfulness, from my inadequacy to his abundant resources.

Remember the story about Jesus crossing the Sea of Galilee in a boat with his disciples? Suddenly a raging storm came up and threatened to capsize the boat. Even though Jesus was asleep, he was aware of it. But it wasn't until they screamed in panic and begged him to help them that he acted. This time he calmed the storm immediately. But it doesn't always happen that way. Sometimes it takes much longer. Sometimes it will take as long as it takes to finally get our eyes on him totally. Believing in him completely to accomplish what he has promised.

God is our refuge and strength,

an ever-present help in trouble.

Psalm 46:1

Immediately the boy's father exclaimed,

"I do believe; help me overcome my unbelief!"

Mark 9:24

If we confess our sins, God is faithful and just and

will forgive us our sins and purify us from all unrighteousness.

1 John 1:9

The LORD is my strength and my shield;

My heart trust in him, and I am helped.

Psalm 28:7

God will deliver the needy who cry out,

    the afflicted who have no one to help.

PSALM 72:12

Here is a trustworthy saying: . . .
If we are faithless,

    Christ will remain faithful,

    for he cannot disown his own.

2 TIMOTHY 2:11, 13

Lord Jesus,

I believe in you. Help my unbelief. Help me hear you more clearly; help me understand you more correctly; help me trust you more completely; help me obey you more reverently. Forgive me for doubting you. Renew my strength. I choose now to obey you as an act of my will, no matter how difficult the circumstances—even though I don't feel like it. My emotions can catch up later. And they will. Thank you, Lord.

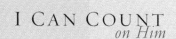

I CAN COUNT
on Him

The sun will rise tomorrow morning—I know it. Even if its arrival is hidden by the clouds, and I can't see it burst over the horizon, I'll still know it's there in the sky right where it's supposed to be. And I can guarantee it will set again in the West, just as it has for centuries.

This "knowing" comes from a lifetime of "seeing." I'm conditioned to believe. My faith in God comes from a lifetime of experiencing him on a day-to-day basis. And as the sun, which God created, does what it's supposed to do day in and day out, so does our Lord. He never stops seeing, never stops loving, never stops being. He just is. Hebrews 13:8 says, "Jesus Christ is the same yesterday and today and forever." What a promise!

The world may change, times may change, tastes and trends may come and go, but the Lord never changes!

Realizing I can count on him gives me hope and courage. It helps me get out of bed in the morning knowing a terrorist bomb could rip through New York City at any moment. It helps me send my children off into an uncertain future. It helps me sleep in peace when there is no peace in this world we live in. It helps me rejoice in my faith that God sees all the chaos and suffering in the world and cares about every bit of it.

I understand the cynics and the pessimists. I would be just like them if I didn't have a personal relationship every minute of every day with a loving God. When people ask, "How could a loving God do such a thing?" I'm amazed that they hold God accountable—rather than the person or groups who actually find joy in the destruction they cause.

God gave us free choice. In Deuteronomy 30:19-20, he says that we can choose life or we can choose death. It is our decision.

When I look at the destruction that has damaged our planet, destroyed bodies and caused so much suffering and death, I am always dismayed that anyone would choose the darkness over the light. But I've also learned that even one simple candle can send the darkness howling. And just one person who truly believes can change the whole world.

The LORD is good and his love endures forever;

his faithfulness continues through all generations.

PSALM 100:5

God, who has called you into fellowship

with his Son Jesus Christ our Lord, is faithful.

1 CORINTHIANS 1:9

The works of God's hands are faithful and just;

all his precepts are trustworthy.

They are steadfast for ever and ever,

done in faithfulness and uprightness.

PSALM 111:7-8

Know therefore that the LORD your God is God;

he is the faithful God, keeping his covenant of love to a thousand

generations of those who love him and keep his commands.

DEUTERONOMY 7:9

Great is your love, higher than the heavens;

your faithfulness reaches to the skies.

PSALM 108:4

The Lord is faithful, and he will

strengthen and protect you from the evil one.

2 THESSALONIANS 3:3

God,

How can I blame you for my sins and evil choices? Heal my spiritual blindness. I need a close encounter of the first kind—with you. I refuse to settle any longer for third rate experiences with phony gods—only you will do, up close and personal. Only you are faithful forever; only you give peace in a crazy world; only you light up the creeping darkness; only you offer hope in despair. Lord, I'm counting on you. Amen

I COME
to the Cross

I Come to the Cross

Bob Somma, Bill Batstone

I come to the cross, seeking mercy and grace
I come to the cross, where You died in my place
Out of my weakness and into Your strength
Humbly, I come to the cross

Your arms are open, You call me by name
You welcome this child that was lost
You paid the price for my guilt and my shame
Jesus, I come
Jesus, I come
Jesus, I come to the cross

WOULD YOU
Be There?

Who came to the cross on that terrible Friday in Jerusalem to witness the crucifixion of Jesus? Who heard him cry out his last, anguished words, "It is finished!" saw the darkness descend, and felt the earth tremble beneath their feet as all heaven mourned the Savior of mankind?

We all know the biblical account of who was physically there—the Roman centurions, several priests of the Sanhedrin, Mary (the Mother of Jesus), Martha, John, and Mary Magdalene, the woman whose life had been transformed by the radical love of a carpenter from Galilee. They were an eclectic group, to say the least.

It wasn't a large crowd—surely much smaller than the mob that had called for Jesus to be crucified. I wonder if he noticed that, except for John, none of his chosen twelve were present?

Who would be standing at the foot of the cross if Jesus were being crucified today? I think the crowd might be surprisingly similar. There would be those who condemn him out of ignorance or jealousy or fear, those who are just curious, those who love to taunt and ridicule for sheer sport with no remorse for their actions, and those who have been truly, eternally, and completely transformed by his *gentle grace.*

Jesus knew every one of them. He looked not only at their actions but also into their hearts. And he knew that the pain he was feeling was for them—the mockers, the curious, and the worshipers alike. He knew that it was for them that he had come.

Would you be there? And if you were, would you be mocking him, cursing him, condemning him, or standing in worshipful silence at the foot of the cross?

I pray that I would have the courage to be there, kneeling at his bleeding feet, shouting out my thanks to him for his sacrifice—the excruciatingly loving gift of his death—for my life.

I come to the cross, the wondrous cross. Won't you?

May I never boast except in the cross of our Lord Jesus Christ,
through which the world has been crucified to me, and I to the world.

GALATIANS 6:14

God forgave us all our sins having canceled the written code,
with its regulations, that was against us and that stood opposed to us;
he took it away, nailing it to the cross.

COLOSSIANS 2:13–14

Let us fix our eyes on Jesus, the author and perfecter of our faith,
who for the joy set before him endured the cross, scorning its shame,
and sat down at the right hand of the throne of God.

HEBREWS 12:2

Christ redeemed us from the curse of the law by becoming a curse
for us, for it is written: "Cursed is everyone who is hung on a tree."

GALATIANS 3:13

Although he was a son, he learned obedience from

what he suffered and once made perfect, he became the source

of eternal salvation for all who obey him.

HEBREWS 5:8-9

It was not with perishable things such as silver or gold

that you were redeemed from the empty way of life handed down

to you from your forefathers, but with the precious blood of Christ,

a lamb without blemish or defect.

1 PETER 1:18-19

Lord Jesus,

It was your power that transformed a bloody cross—an instrument of death—into a source of eternal life. It was your love that caused you to offer your innocence in exchange for my guilt—on that cross. It was your blood that satisfied God's holiness and unleashed his grace—on that cross. Thank you, Lord, for enduring the cross that I might embrace it. Amen.

PEACE

PEACE

Kathie Lee Gifford, Phil Sillas

You can hear the thunder, the clamour and the roar
The whole world's marching in the streets
Against—or for—the war

While I sit in the silence of a worn, but steady heart
With a peace inside my spirit only heaven can impart

A peace that passes all understanding
Commanding every storm cloud to clear
Is ours if we trust in Him
Put our faith just in Him
His perfect love will cast out all fear
A peace that reaches past worldly reason
Even as the world is losing its mind
A peace that can't be defined
A peace only He designed
We'll find if we trust in Him

Put our faith just in Him ... peace

You can hear the shouting, the screaming at each other
As nation after nation rises up against another

While I sit in calm assurance that the war's already won
With a peace inside my spirit that only God's will will be done

So as the battle rages and as the innocent die
And the whole world cries in agony
Shake their fists and wonder "why?"
We who call Him Father can rest in perfect peace
His perfect love casts out all fear
His wonders never cease

WHO I AM

People often ask how I can be a believer while working in a world like show business. I always respond the same way: How could I not? I can't imagine enduring the discouragement, the rejection, or the instability, not to mention the judgments of the media without knowing *exactly* who I am.

You see, I may work as an actress, singer, writer, or talk show host—but those things don't define who I *am;* they only describe what I *do.* Who I *am* is God's beloved child. He knows me, everything about me, because he created me. And he alone determines my value—my intrinsic worth—not some opinion poll or gossip columnist. Knowing that brings me peace—peace of mind and peace of heart.

That is so important when I'm facing difficult times, when I'm misunderstood, when I feel rejected or defamed. I know that I am God's child and he loves me despite my mistakes, my imperfections, my blind spots. He loves me unconditionally—throughout the stormy places in my life.

Jesus put it this way to his followers: "I have told you these things, so that in me you may have peace. In this world you will have trouble. But take heart! I have overcome the world" (John 16:33).

Are you experiencing God's peace? You certainly don't have to be in show business to obtain it. It comes from giving your life to him and walking through each day with him as a child would with a loving father. It comes with a solid understanding of *who* you are—God's precious child!

I know that God can surround you with peace in any and every circumstance. I know because I experience his peace every day. It is a peace that surpasses my understanding and calms my hurts and fears. It's a peace that can be yours as well just for the asking.

Jesus said, "Peace I leave with you." How I wish I could leave such a gift with the people I love!

How great is the love the Father has lavished on us,

that we should be called children of God! And that is what we are!

1   J O H N   3 : 1

"I will be a Father to you,

and you will be my sons and daughters,

says the Lord Almighty."

2   C O R I N T H I A N S   6 : 1 8

To all who received Christ, to those who believed in his name, he gave

the right to become children of God—children born not of natural descent,

nor of human decision or a husband's will, but born of God.

J O H N   1 : 1 2 – 1 3

You will keep in perfect peace

him whose mind is steadfast,

because he trusts in you, Lord.

I S A I A H   2 6 : 3

In everything by prayer and petition, with thanksgiving, present your requests to God. And the peace of God, which transcends all understanding, will guard your hearts and your minds in Christ Jesus.

PHILIPPIANS 4:6–7

I will listen to what God the LORD will say; he promises peace to his people, his saints.

PSALM 85:8

God,

You know everything—so you know how crazy my life is right now. I feel like I'm losing control. Please give me your peace. Strengthen my mind and heart in the face of constant criticism and lack of affirmation. Thank you for validating me through your unconditional love. Fill me with your spirit, and make me an instrument of your peace.

IN THE MIDST
of a Storm

There are many different ways to describe that dark, lonely place we sometimes find ourselves in. Some call it the desert or the night or the pit. For me the imagery of a storm always comes to mind.

The irony is that I love to experience storms when I am protected from them. They're really quite beautiful and thrilling. But a storm that is experienced without protection can be a terribly frightening thing. Now when

I go through those difficult, painful times in my life, I try to remember that even though the wind is wailing and the tide is high and treacherous, I am protected! That's the confidence I have in him. "God has said, 'Never will I leave you; never will I forsake you'"(Hebrews 13:5).

And you can have that same assurance.

All you have to do to feel that you are not alone during a storm is to turn to the Psalms and read about David crying out to the Lord. What stormy times he experienced! And yet he was able to confidently proclaim in Psalm 23: "Though I walk through the valley of the shadow of death, I will fear no evil, for you are with me."

I have known this scripture since I was a little girl, but I experienced the truth of it during my beloved daddy's last days. He had been sick for several years and he seemed to disappear before our eyes as his body became decimated and his mind became debilitated from the disease.

And yet my daddy never complained, never cried out in anger or despair—just quietly and courageously accepted God's will for his life. As the time grew nearer for him to go "home" to heaven, a peace descended upon our house and everyone in it. We circled his bed, ministering to his needs and singing hymns of thanksgiving and praise. During those hours, we never stopped holding him, hugging and kissing him, and praying for him. We all noticed a serenity about his demeanor. We could only describe it as "other-worldly." After he died the hospice workers told us it was the most peaceful passing they had ever witnessed. We knew why.

God's promises are true. We can depend on them because he cannot lie. Colossians 3:16 says, "Let Christ's word with all its wisdom and richness live in you" (God's Word).

God has said,

> *"Never will I leave you;*
>
> *never will I forsake you."*

So we say with confidence,

> *"The Lord is my helper, I will not be afraid."*

HEBREWS 13:5–6

Let the peace of Christ rule in your hearts, since as members of one body you were called to peace. And be thankful.

COLOSSIANS 3:15

The LORD is close to the brokenhearted;

> *and saves those who are crushed in spirit.*

PSALM 34:18

To each one of us grace has been given as Christ apportioned it.

EPHESIANS 4:7

We know that if the earthly tent we live in is destroyed,
we have a building from God, an eternal house in heaven,
not built by human hands.

2 CORINTHIANS 5:1

God of Peace,

The power to calm a storm at sea is pretty impressive. Your disciples asked, "Who is this man that even the wind and sea obey him?" Lord, calm the storms raging in my life. Be my peacemaker, my prince of peace; and grant me "the peace of God that surpasses all understanding, guarding my heart and mind in Christ Jesus." Thank you, Lord, that peace is not the absence of problems—but the presence of God. Amen.

WRESTLING
with the Mist

Have you ever quarreled with God? I know I have. Years ago my sister, Michie, had to have an illiostomy performed in order to save her life. She was 23, the beautiful mother of a brand new baby girl. Such an operation requires the attachment of a plastic bag to the abdomen for the collection of the bowel—not sexy stuff by anyone's standards and especially difficult for a person so young and newly married.

On the day of her surgery, Michie experienced three grandmal seizures, and we were warned that she might not survive. As she lay in a coma, I sat by her side in the hospital room arguing with God. I told him exactly what I thought of him and his so called "loving kindness." At that moment, my love and concern for my sister were greater than my trust in God. Eventually, my sister opened her eyes and saw me there, sobbing. I will never forget her words.

"Kathie," she whispered, "Don't curse God because of this bag. I thank him for it because it means I get to live the rest of my life." Her courage and faith in the midst of pain and loss were astounding. I felt shamed and humbled.

In 1996, I went through another difficult time. Incredibly, I was being accused of abusing children in foreign sweat shops. I couldn't see God in that at all, and once again cried out before him. Eventually he helped me get my eyes off of myself and onto the children who truly do work under horribly abusive conditions in certain parts of the world. Even though those children had no connection to me, surrendering my anger to God and placing my hand in his enabled me to marshal my resources on their behalf. Laws and conditions that had been in place for more than one hundred years were amended and the victims of abuse were helped.

We wrestle with the mist when we wrestle with God. Only by our surrender to his will do we ever find the peace that passes all understanding. Trust him—even in your darkest hour—and he will help you see the sunshine through the rain.

We know that in all things God works for the good of those
who love him, who have been called according to his purpose.

ROMANS 8:28

Submit to God and be at peace with him;
in this way prosperity will come to you.
Accept instruction from his mouth
and lay up his words in your heart.

JOB 22:21–22

Man's anger does not bring about the righteous life that God desires.

JAMES 1:20

Be joyful always; pray continually; give thanks
in all circumstances, for this is God's will for you in Christ Jesus.

1 THESSALONIANS 5:16–18

Wise men turn away anger.

PROVERBS 29:8

Who are you, O man, to talk back to God? "Shall what is formed say to him who formed it, 'Why did you make me like this?'"

ROMANS 9:20

God of Peace,

I'm amazed that the perfect, all-knowing, all-powerful God is willing to take the heat from imperfect, weak creatures like me—full of my criticisms, complaints, and fears. And still, you offer me your peace, which like yourself, is beyond my understanding—even guarding my heart and mind in life's most vulnerable, scary moments. I trust in you. Amen.

TO PLEASE
You

To Please You

Shirley Bunnell

Before I come into Your presence
Before I enter in and worship You
Soften my heart
Open my eyes
To the things I need to see
To the things You have for me
To the things that will only please You, Lord
How I want to please You, Lord

To please You, Lord
I want to please You, Lord
And do only what you would have me do today

MY INSPIRATION

One of my great advantages in life is also one of my greatest disadvantages. I am a people pleaser. I like to make people happy, and admittedly, I want them to like me in return. There's nothing inherently wrong with that except at times it takes my eyes off the one who truly deserves my praise, devotion, and love. I don't seem to find time in my day to go to that still, quiet place in the Lord's presence and dwell there.

The irony is that my time with the Lord is the very thing that enables me to give my best to others. It is the spiritual—time with God— that inspires my physical and emotional well-being. I forget that, as do many Christians.

You see, God created us in his image. Like him, we are triune, with physical, emotional, and spiritual aspects to our being. We spend a great deal of time taking care of our physical needs—eating, sleeping, bathing (and what my daughter calls, "fluffing"). We also spend lots of energy on our emotional needs—reading, going to therapy, studying, conversing, and working.

Most of us work hard to keep all our plates spinning, and yet, many people—even Christians—say they feel empty on the inside. That's a sure sign that spiritual needs have not been met.

The best days of my life are the days when I properly balance all three dimensions of my being. Those are the days I feel most in sync with nature, at peace in my soul, inspired in my work, and excited and challenged to be a light in the world.

Light a candle in your world by setting aside that quiet, special time to listen to the voice of God in your heart. Let him refresh and renew you as you read his word, give him your burdens through prayer, and spend time meditating on his love and care.

I will meditate on all your works

and consider all your mighty deeds, Lord.

PSALM 77:12

Jesus said, "Seek first God's kingdom and his righteousness,

and all these things will be given to you as well."

MATTHEW 6:33

The LORD said, "My Presence will go with you,

and I will give you rest."

EXODUS 33:14

Blessed are those who have learned to acclaim you,

who walk in the light of your presence, O LORD.

PSALM 89:15

You have made known to me the path of life, O Lord;

you will fill me with joy in your presence,

with eternal pleasures at your right hand.

PSALM 16:11

"You will call upon me and come and pray to me,

and I will listen to you. You will seek me and find me when

you seek me with all your heart," says the Lord.

JEREMIAH 29:12-13

Heavenly Father,

You have created all of me, all of the aspects of my being. Teach me to keep them in balance, giving time each day to take care of my body, enrich my mind, and find my inspiration in the holy stillness of your presence. Then my life will be pleasing to you and also to others. Amen.

HE GIVETH
More Grace

HE GIVETH MORE GRACE

Annie Johnson Flint and Hubert Mitchell

He giveth more grace when the burdens grow greater
He sendeth more strength when the labors increase
To added affliction He addeth His mercy
To multiplied trials, His multiplied peace

His love has no limit, His grace has no measure
His power has no boundary known unto men
For out of His infinite riches in Jesus
He giveth, and giveth, and giveth again

When we have exhausted our store of endurance
When our strength has failed ere the day is half done
When we reach the end of our hoarded resources
Our Father's full giving is only begun

KATHIE LEE GIFFORD 73

MORE THAN *Enough*

We all have certain songs that are special to us. This beautiful old hymn, "He Giveth More Grace," stirred my soul and moved me to tears the first time I heard it years ago—it still does.

It was at a movie theater in Annapolis, Maryland, almost forty years ago, that I asked Jesus into my heart. As I watched the Billy Graham film, "The Restless Ones," I discovered an important truth: God loves me!

In that tender, transforming moment, I made a decision that colored every decision I have made since—to receive God's love.

Through the years, I've come to understand a great deal more about God's love—and his *grace,* which made his love available to me.

Grace, as defined in Webster's dictionary means "unmerited favor." It is an undeserved gift. All have sinned and fallen short of God's glory—or his standard for "righteousness." The very best person who ever lived does not deserve heaven. Only Jesus lived a completely pure, holy life. So it is God's grace—his love combined with his compassion for us—that looks beyond our sin to our potential to be God's sons and daughters. Then he *gives us more grace* so that we might live meaningful lives here on earth and have a blessed and expected end in heaven.

Have you heard the good news that God loves you? Have you made a decision to receive that love? God is reaching out to you—reach back. Don't leave God's precious gift of salvation through Jesus Christ laying unopened. Receive his grace. And as the years go by, you will see that he will give you more grace, and more, and more until that day when you finish your course and walk worshipfully into his presence.

From the fullness of God's grace,
we have all received one blessing after another.

JOHN 1:16

God is able to make all grace abound to you, so that in all things
at all times, having all that you need, you will abound in every good work.

2 CORINTHIANS 9:8

You know the grace of our Lord Jesus Christ, that though
he was rich, yet for your sakes he became poor, so that you through
his poverty might become rich.

2 CORINTHIANS 8:9

Grace and peace be yours in abundance
through the knowledge of God and of Jesus our Lord.

2 PETER 1:2

The Lord said to me, "My grace is sufficient for you,
for my power is made perfect in weakness."

2 CORINTHIANS 12:9

The God of all grace, who called you to his eternal glory in Christ,
after you have suffered a little while,
will himself restore you and make you strong, firm, and steadfast.

1 PETER 5:10

Gracious God,

Thank you for the grace that brought your love to me. What's so amazing about grace is that it really is God's Riches At Christ's Expense. You didn't owe me your grace, and I certainly could not have earned it. Your precious Son, Jesus, provided it for me. My job is to receive it—and I do! Amen.

THE MEASURE
of My Life

THE MEASURE OF MY LIFE

Kathie Lee Gifford, Phil Sillas

I hear Your voice
I have a choice
Will I listen or will I turn away
Follow my heart
Or surrender to Your will
You're the potter, I am just the clay

I see Your hand
Help me understand
As we travel this journey, Lord, I pray
Ignore the world
And follow in Your way
I desire to shadow You today

For the world has much to offer
But it's of very little worth
And it's easy to be blinded
By the riches of this earth
But if my treasure is in heaven
Then my heart will be there too
And the measure of my life
Will be what I give back to You

I know Your word
And I have heard
You have promised your children can be free
From all the pains, and the chains
That bind in every way
Loving Lord, free us all today

NO REGRETS

My father wasn't rich or famous. He didn't have a trophy room to remind him of all his accomplishments, and yet I doubt I will ever meet anyone who lived a more splendid life. When he died on November 19, 2002, I doubt that he had even one regret. I can see him standing before the Lord and hearing the words: "Well done, my good and faithful servant."

In my opinion, *that* is the real measure of a life. I know billionaires—individuals with great wealth and celebrity. Although they seem to have everything, a great many of them leave nothing of lasting value in their wake.

I recently turned 50 and found myself for the first time examining my past rather than dreaming about my future. On the surface at least, I have lived a successful life. But I needed to know that my success went below the surface. I began to reflect on the years I had wasted, the decisions that were fool-hardy, the deep hurts I hadn't truly dealt with, the disappointments that still sting. I put them all on the table and took a good look at them. Then I asked God to help me answer the questions: *What will I do with the rest of my life? Am I investing my life in eternal treasure? Am I working to build a godly legacy for my children as my father did for his?*

It's always a bit of a shock to realize that you're in the latter portion of your life. But soon enough the shock fades, and it's time to stop and evaluate where your life is headed. Will you be remembered as a person of character, someone who lived a life pleasing to God? When you stand before God's throne, will you hear the words my father heard, "Well done, my good and faithful servant"?

It's never too early or too late to take the measure of your life. And if you don't like what you see, ask God to forgive you and help you make changes that will ensure a life without regrets and a gracious legacy for those who follow you.

Who is wise and understanding among you? Let him show it
by his good life, by deeds done in the humility that comes from wisdom.

JAMES 3:13

Our conscience testifies that we have conducted ourselves in the world,
and especially in our relations with you, in the holiness
and sincerity that are from God. We have done so not according
to worldly wisdom but according to God's grace.

2 CORINTHIANS 1:12

The world and its desires pass away,
but the man who does the will of God lives forever.

1 JOHN 2:17

Be transformed by the renewing of your mind.
Then you will be able to test and approve what God's will is—
his good, pleasing, and perfect will.

ROMANS 12:2

Store up for yourselves treasures in heaven, where moth and rust

do not destroy, and where thieves do not break in

and steal. For where your treasure is, there your heart will be also.

MATTHEW 6:20–21

Forgetting what is behind and straining toward what is ahead,

I press on toward the goal to win the prize

for which God has called me heavenward in Christ Jesus.

PHILIPPIANS 3:13–14

Dear Lord,

You know that part of me is far more interested in acquiring earthly treasure than seeking your kingdom. Forgive me, Lord. Strengthen me by your Spirit, and help me set my priorities aright. Each day, I pray that you will remind me that a true and lasting legacy does not consist of the possessions of a lifetime—but the power of a life well-lived. Amen.

GOD USES THOSE
He Chooses

For the past four years, I have been writing a musical based on the life of Aimee Semple McPherson, an evangelist who, during the 1920s and 1930s, was one of the most celebrated and controversial women of her day.

Aimee was a servant of God who defied the social, religious, and cultural norms of the times and achieved enormous and unprecedented success. It is also true that she died young and alone in a hotel room from an accidental overdose of barbiturates. She seemed to be such a contradiction in terms. Devout, on one hand; twice divorced and remarried, on the other. She was both one of the most powerful women ever in the pulpit, yet often weak and vulnerable in affairs of the heart. She seemed to bounce from super-woman to frail, fragile, and flawed.

As I continued to work on the musical, it occurred to me that God will use *anyone* who is willing to serve him. He does not care at all what the world thinks of his choices. Perhaps, God works best with those who know they can accomplish very little on their own and therefore, acknowledge their need for him.

Someone once told me the best way to describe 'ego' was like this: *Edging God Out*—thinking we don't need him and going out on our own, in our own strength. Here's the thing about our own strength—it doesn't last! Even a triathlete with the heart of a stallion will one day stop running.

We are human with human limitations and only when we rely on God will we be able to accomplish all that he has called us to do.

What has God called you to do? Does it seem insurmountable, impossible to accomplish on your own? In 2 Corinthians 1:9–10, Paul wrote: "We felt like we'd been sent to death row, that it was all over for us. As it turned out, it was the best thing that could have happened. Instead of trusting in our own strength or wits to get out of it, we were forced to trust God totally—not a bad idea since he's the God who raises the dead! And he did it, rescued us from certain doom. And he'll do it again, rescuing us as many times as we need rescuing" (THE MESSAGE).

Put yourself and your calling in the mighty hands of God. That's what Aimee Semple McPherson did. She understood that her worldly success didn't matter to the Lord. But she did. At the end of the musical, she sings a song of longing called, "I Want To Matter."

"I want to matter, before I am gone
To have once been the shoulder that someone leaned on
To have been the safe harbour in someone's sad storm
To know someone was blessed, because I was born."

A life lived for God's glory is a life well-lived.

In our hearts we felt the sentence of death.

But this happened that we might not rely on ourselves but on God.

2 CORINTHIANS 1:9

I can do everything through Christ who gives me strength.

PHILIPPIANS 4:13

Do not fear, for I am with you;

do not be dismayed, for I am your God.

I will strengthen you and help you;

I will uphold you with my righteous right hand.

ISAIAH 41:10

My flesh and my heart may fail,

but God is the strength of my heart

and my portion forever.

PSALM 73:26

The Lord gives strength to the weary

and increases the power of the weak.

May God strengthen your hearts so that you will be

blameless and holy in the presence of our God and Father when

our Lord Jesus comes with all his holy ones.

1 THESSALONIANS 3:13

Mighty God,

What can I say? Thanks for choosing to love me, when I was unlovable. Thanks for finding me when I couldn't find myself. Thanks for affirming me, for giving me significance—when I doubted my own self worth. So I surrender my small life to you. I want my life to matter; I want to make a difference. Lord, you're on record using weak things, despised things, common things, powerless things—so use me. Amen.

GENTLE
Grace

GENTLE GRACE

Kathie Lee Gifford, Phil Sillas

Tender Saviour, gracious Lord
How can I express
My grateful heart for all you do
How You love, how You lead, how You bless

Gentle Saviour, loving Lord
How can I repay
The debt I owe for all You've done
Every moment, every hour, everyday

Gentle grace, gentle grace
Amazing, tender, gentle grace
I lift my hands, lift up my face
To thank all of heaven
For Your love and Your gentle grace

Tender Jesus, gracious King
Receive my gift of praise
Look beyond my broken heart
Father, look at the offering I raise

A LIVING
Relationship

I think one of the biggest misconceptions in our culture is that there is no difference between religion and faith. In my opinion, they are completely different. Look at what is happening in many parts of the world. Religious zealots, in a misguided attempt to obtain martyrdom, are strapping explosives to their bodies and blowing themselves up. The more "infidels" they can take with them, the more successful their effort, and the more pride their families have in them.

Religion blows people up with hatred. Faith fills people up with love. First John 4:16-17 says, "God is love. Whoever lives in love lives in God, and God in him. In this way, love is made complete among us so that we will have confidence on the day of judgment, because in this world we are like him."

A person of faith—someone who truly has been touched of God—is filled with his love, because God himself is love. This love enables them to care for, serve, and forgive others. It enables them to pray for their enemies and "turn the other cheek." True faith is radical—it transforms a human being from the inside out. They become instruments of peace rather than instruments of judgment or destruction.

When people say to me, "Oh, I've heard you're really religious," I cringe. I am not religious at all. I am faith-filled. Religion is a dogma of restrictions and regulations. Faith is a living relationship with a living and loving God that frees up the believer to achieve all things through his power.

I try to live a life of faith as a testimony to the Holy Spirit that lives within me. I consider myself blessed to have been introduced to such a life force so many years ago. And it is because of God's great mercy to me, his gentle grace, in spite of my own imperfections, that I am able to experience love and compassion for others.

Religion that God our Father accepts as pure and faultless is this:
to look after orphans and widows in their distress and to keep oneself
from being polluted by the world.

JAMES 1:27

Jesus said, "All men will
know that you are my disciples,
if you love one another."

JOHN 13:35

Jesus said, "Love your enemies and pray for those who persecute you,
that you may be sons of your Father in heaven."

MATTHEW 5:44–45

Whoever loves his brother lives in the light,
and there is nothing in him to make him stumble.

1 JOHN 2:10

It is written: "I believed; therefore I have spoken."
With that same spirit of faith we also believe and therefore speak
because we know that the one who raised
the Lord Jesus from the dead will also raise us with Jesus and
present us with you in his presence.

2 CORINTHIANS 4:13–14

All a man's ways seem right to him,
but the LORD weighs the heart.

PROVERBS 21:2

Loving Father, Son, and Holy Spirit,

Create a beautiful and powerful spiritual harmony in my life. Renew my mind with truth; liberate my heart with love; sanctify my spirit with holiness; educate my will for obedience; transform my lifestyle into radical righteousness. And Lord, since you promise to be the solid rock in our living relationship—I gratefully promise to be the weakest link. Thanks.

THE TWO THIEVES

I have often wondered about the two thieves who were crucified alongside Jesus. They are so representative of the freedom of choice we are given as human beings. Both were guilty of their crimes and both were judged accordingly. But each views the innocent man next to him differently. One thief rejects Jesus, while the other embraces him. One of them taunts and ridicules, while the other cries out for mercy.

Many people feel that a believer must be baptized with water in order to enter the Kingdom of God. Others feel a believer must be baptized with the Holy Spirit. But this account—the last in Christ's earthly life—demonstrates to me that all a person has to do to enter the Kingdom of God is simply *believe.*

"Jesus," the repentant thief cried out in anguish—"Remember me when you come into your Kingdom."

And even in his agony Jesus responded in grace. "Truly," he told the thief, "you shall be with me today in Paradise." God's mercy was equally available to the two men, but only one chose to receive it. Jesus didn't force his message on the unbelieving thief.

I have friends who are wonderful, loving people, but their hearts are hardened to the gospel. I can't imagine how they can resist God's message of love and mercy—but they continue to do so, and I can't make that decision for them. All I can do is continue to love them and pray that their eyes will be opened to the gift of grace that has been laid at their feet.

Very little is recorded about the lives of the two thieves who hung on crosses next to Jesus. But we do know this: One opened his heart and received God's gift of eternal life. The other did not. What will you do with God's wonderful and gracious gift?

Jesus said, "I tell you the truth,

he who believes has everlasting life."

J O H N   6 : 4 7

If you confess with your mouth, "Jesus is Lord,"

and believe in your heart that God raised him from the dead, you will

be saved. For it is with your heart that you believe and are justified,

and it is with your mouth that you confess and are saved.

R O M A N S   1 0 : 9 - 1 0

Whoever believes in Jesus is not condemned.

J O H N   3 : 1 8

All the prophets testify about Christ that everyone

who believes in him receives forgiveness of sins through his name.

A C T S   1 0 : 4 3

Jesus said," I am the resurrection and the life.

He who believes in me will live, even though he dies; and whoever lives

and believes in me will never die. Do you believe this?"

JOHN 11:25-26

This is love: not that we loved God, but that he loved us

and sent his Son as an atoning sacrifice for our sins.

1 JOHN 4:10

O God,

We are all dead men walking. And yet your gentle grace offers us paradise. But will I choose life? Will I choose Christ? Freedom—what a wonderful and terrible gift. Thank you for not asking me to earn your love, or to live a perfect life, or to deserve your forgiveness. Lord, you prayed, "Father, forgive them." You ask only for my faith. Jesus, remember me. Amen.

I LOVE YOU, *Lord*

I LOVE YOU, LORD

Laurie Klein

I love You, Lord and I lift my voice
To worship You, O my soul rejoice
Take joy, my King, in what You hear
May it be a sweet, sweet sound
In Your ear.

LET GOD
Lead the Way

When I was a child growing up under my parents' humble roof, I felt rich. I was loved, I was rocked, hugged, and kissed. I was fed, bathed, sung to, listened to, and encouraged to be everything and anything I could ever be.

Today, I look at my children while they are playing, sleeping, wrestling, playing the piano—and I delight in them. I love looking after them, drying their tears, and sharing their little triumphs.

I have come to realize our heavenly Father feels the same way when he watches us—his children. He loves us and delights in us. He longs for us to know him and fellowship with him. And just like we have plans and dreams for our children, God has plans and dreams for us.

When I left "Live with Regis and Kathie Lee," in July of 2000, many people thought I had some elaborate plan all mapped out for my future. They couldn't have been more wrong! I had no idea what I was going to do next. I just knew in my heart that God, my Father, would counsel and guide me until I found my way.

And I was right. God opened up a brand new, exciting world of musical theater for me. I can stay at home and write, record the demo music in the recording studio in our house, and still have dinner with my family and tuck my kids into bed at night! Once again, I was reminded that God loves me and has a wonderful plan for my life.

It's possible that you did not grow up in a loving home like I did. It may not be easy for you to believe that God could love you. But I can tell you with certainty that he does. He delights in you, and he is eager to help you fulfill the purpose for which he created you.

Place your trust in God. Let him guide you through the uncertainties of this life. Like a loving Father, he will look after you and always lead and guide you. Count on him and you will never be disappointed.

God demonstrates his own love for us in this:
While we were still sinners, Christ died for us.

ROMANS 5:8

Because of his great love for us, God, who is rich in mercy,
made us alive with Christ even when we were dead in transgressions—
it is by grace you have been saved.

EPHESIANS 2:4–5

This is how we know what love is: Jesus Christ laid down his life for us.
And we ought to lay down our lives for our brothers.

1 JOHN 3:16

Jesus said, "He who loves me will be loved by my Father,
and I too will love him and show myself to him."

JOHN 14:21

The Lord is full of compassion and mercy.

JAMES 5:11

God is love. Whoever lives in love lives in God, and God in him.
In this way, love is made complete among us so that we will have
confidence on the day of judgment, because in this world we are like him.

1 JOHN 4:16–17

Heavenly Father,

How could I resist your love? I see it in every part of my life—even those parts that are challenging me right now. In good times, in bad times, your loving presence is always with me. Thank you, Lord. Help me to be an instrument of your love to others. Amen.

MAGNIFICENT
Obsession

Remember how wonderful you felt when you first fell in love? Your every moment was spent thinking of that person, missing him, longing for him. And when you were together, your every moment was spent trying to please him, enjoy his company, caress him, and get as close to him as you possibly could.

God wants us to have that kind of "magnificent obsession" with him. He is the lover of our souls, but there is nothing sadder than unrequited love. It's not enough that he loves us—God wants us to love him back in the same way. He is a jealous God.

In John 15:9, Jesus says, "As the Father has loved me, so have I loved you. Now remain in my love." He also describes himself as a "bridegroom." Remember the joy you experienced on your wedding day? It was indescribable, wasn't it? Knowing that you were going to spend the rest of your earthly life with that wonderful, loving, "practically" perfect person gave your future a hope and even a thrill!

It's all too easy for relationships to grow dull and boring with time, and that has happened to me many times in my "marriage" to the Lord. But it's always *my fault!* I am always the one who has moved away, or stopped communicating, or allowed other things or other people to take my time and devotion. But there is hope! Psalm 32:1 says, "What happiness for those whose guilt has been forgiven! What relief for those who have confessed their sins and God has cleared their record" (TLB).

Someone once explained it to me this way: A loving couple is driving in the car. They are sitting very close to one another as they travel along. Eventually the day comes when the passenger says to the driver, "Remember the good times when we used to be so close?" To which the driver answers, "Yes, but I didn't move."

It's a great analogy for our walk of faith with the Lord. If we don't feel that loving, tender, closeness we once had, it is because we have moved away—not him. Fall in love again!

Come near to God and he will come near to you.

Jesus said, "Love the Lord your God with all your heart and with all your soul and with all your mind and with all your strength."

Jesus said, "As the Father has loved me, so have I loved you. Now remain in my love."

Jesus said, "All that the Father gives me will come to me, and whoever comes to me I will never drive away."

Praise be to the God and Father of our Lord Jesus Christ,
who ... chose us in him before the creation
of the world to be holy and blameless in his sight.

EPHESIANS 1:3

The LORD is near to all who call on him,
to all who call on him in truth.

PSALM 145:18

Loving God,

I need spiritual passion. I want a life-changing, spiritual love affair with my creator and redeemer. Lord, free me to love you with all my heart, soul, strength, and mind. Whatever is blocking my love, remove it. I repent of it. Lord Jesus, right now, I renew my vows. "I do." Amen.

WHAT THE
Master Wants

Humility is a lost art in our culture today. Everywhere we look it seems that arrogance and haughtiness and pride are rewarded, and anyone who is humble is considered weak and powerless.

But God honors a humble heart. The Bible says that "A pretentious, showy life is an empty life; a plain and simple life is a full life." (Proverbs 13:7 THE MESSAGE)

But how can we live a simple life in the midst of such a complicated, fast-paced world? There are so many distractions, so many temptations, so many opportunities!

We can do what Paul tells us to do in Ephesians 5:17, *"Don't live carelessly, unthinkingly. Make sure you understand what the Master wants."* (The Message)

The Master wants me. He wants you. And not just the convenient part—the whole part . . . the sum of all parts! Or as my kids would say, "the whole enchilada."

And he deserves no less. The grace he has shed on us as individuals is beyond measure. And in spite of our lack of gratitude, he continues to give us more and more and more.

Would you keep giving wonderful gifts to someone who never thanked you? Never acknowledged you? Ignored you? Ridiculed you? Rejected you? Of course not. But God, our heavenly Father, does.

I have always insisted that my children say, "thank you." So much so that now my kids will lean over and say, "Mom, that lady didn't say 'thank you.'" They notice. Imagine how much God notices!

It's so easy to make a list of our grievances and our complaints. But how often do we make a list of the countless blessings our Lord has graciously given us? How often do we even acknowledge a beautiful sunrise, or a rose bush in full bloom, or a warm breeze on our weary faces and say "thank you, Lord"? We can never out give God. But we can sure try.

Do not think of yourself more highly than you ought,
but rather think of yourself with sober judgment, in accordance
with the measure of faith God has given you.

Humility and the fear of the LORD
bring wealth and honor and life.

PROVERBS 22:4

Humble yourselves before the Lord, and he will lift you up.

JAMES 4:10

Clothe yourselves with humility toward one another, because,
"God opposes the proud
but gives grace to the humble."
Humble yourselves, therefore, under God's mighty hand,
that he may lift you up in due time.

1 PETER 5:5–6

The LORD sustains the humble

but casts the wicked to the ground.

PSALM 147:6

God guides the humble in what is right

and teaches them his way.

PSALM 25:9

Gracious God,

How can I say thanks? I humble myself before you, and rejoice in your lordship. I delight to be under your authority. Whatever you want, Lord Jesus, here's my life— take all of me. Amen.

GLORIFY
Thy Name

GLORIFY THY NAME

Donna Adkins

Father, we love You
We worship and adore You
Glorify Thy name in all the earth
Glorify Thy name
Glorify Thy name
Glorify Thy name in all the earth

Jesus, we love You
We worship and adore You
Glorify Thy name in all the earth
Glorify Thy name
Glorify Thy name
Glorify Thy name in all the earth

Spirit, we love You
We worship and adore You
Glorify Thy name in all the earth
Glorify Thy name
Glorify Thy name
Glorify Thy name in all the earth

CHOOSING
to Love Him

It's ironic to think that the God of the universe longs for anything at all—but he does! He longs with all his being to fellowship with his followers and hear their songs of worship and praise. And he wants them to worship him truly from their spirits. "A time is coming and has now come when the true worshipers will worship the Father in spirit and truth, for they are the kind of worshipers the Father seeks. God is spirit, and his worshipers must worship in spirit and in truth" (John 4:23–24).

Jesus often pointed out the difference between a "religious" person and a truly spiritual person of faith. Once in a parable Jesus talked about a poor widow who gave everything she had into the temple treasury, while a rich man was making a big showing of putting his large gift on the altar. Jesus praised the poor widow for giving her all. Jesus was trying to say that we should be placing our lives on the altar. We need to make the sacrifice of our whole being in order to truly please him. "Offer yourselves to God, as those who have been brought from death to life" (Romans 6:13).

Our Creator could have manufactured us as complete robots who mechanically go about our lives obeying his commands and doing his bidding. But that would not have fulfilled his desire for the love he has shown to be returned to him. That would have been nothing but cold religion.

I can't imagine raising children who do exactly what I tell them to with a "yes, Ma'am," "at your service, Ma'am," attitude but never crawl into my lap and cuddle, or blow bubbles with me in the bathtub or take long walks with me on a beautiful spring morning.

Romans 12:1 says, "Take your everyday, ordinary life—your sleeping, eating, going to work, and walking around life—and place it before God as an offering" (The Message). God wants more than our cold, clinical obedience; he wants praise and devotion that comes from our hearts.

There is a common misconception in our culture today that a life of faith is a boring life: a kind of boot camp life full of rules and regulations that is joyless, routine, humorless. But nothing is further from the truth. People confuse "religious" with "spiritual" and that is because too often Christians have acted that way. We have been self-righteous when we should have been humble. We have been judgmental when we should have been loving. And we have been exclusive when we should have been inclusive of the world around us.

It's a lot easier to hide behind our church doors, and safely sing our hymns and pray our prayers than it is to make our lives a living sacrifice— as he did—to bring glory to our Father. It's a lot easier to give to missions than to go on one.

Come, let us bow down in worship,

let us kneel before the LORD our Maker;

for he is our God

and we are the people of his pasture,

the flock under his care.

PSALM 95:6-7

This is what the LORD says—

"Fear not, for I have redeemed you;

I have summoned you by name; you are mine."

ISAIAH 43:1

For the sake of his great name the LORD will not reject his people,

because the LORD was pleased to make you his own.

1 SAMUEL 12:22

The LORD takes delight in his people;

he crowns the humble with salvation.

PSALM 149:4

Know that the LORD is God.

    It is he who made us, and we are his;

    we are his people, the sheep of his pasture.

PSALM 100:3

    You are a chosen people, a royal priesthood, a holy nation,

a people belonging to God, that you may declare the praises of him

    who called you out of darkness into his wonderful light.

1 PETER 2:9

God,

You are a major risk taker. Why would you grant your creatures the freedom to say no? Perhaps for the joy of hearing them say yes! I choose to worship you in spirit and in truth. I choose to offer my life as a living sacrifice. Jesus, I choose to love you. Yes, Lord!

FINALLY

FINALLY

Kathie Lee Gifford, Phil Sillas

You can search the whole world over
Discover every four-leaf clover
You can store up new treasures
You can seek out new pleasures
Collect new friends of every kind

You can climb every mountain you're able
And dine with kings at their table
You can sail every ocean, pledge your devotion
But you will eventually find

That nothing will fill your sky
Or satisfy your every longing
Nothing will thrill your soul
Or give you a sense of belonging
Life will keep aching
Your heart will keep breaking
And time will keep taking its toll

Until you finally find Him
Until you finally find Him

You can read every book on your shelf
Conquer the world by yourself
You can solve every mystery
Create your own history
Write every song that comes to mind
You can dream your dreams into existence

You can choose any path, go the distance
You can run from the thunder
Embrace any wonder
But still you'll eventually find...

Oh don't you long to give up the game
Surrender the struggle and call Him by name
Fall at His feet
And finally be free
So blinded by love
You can finally see

A CERTAIN
Outcome

The Bible says, "God is the author and finisher of our faith." He alone knows how all the twists and turns of our lives will come together. That's because he has had a master plan in place since before the beginning of time. Each life plan is different, unique, personal. But one thing is sure, at the *end* of our earthly lives, there is a certain outcome waiting.

Our heavenly Father must feel great joy when our earthly lives end and he welcomes us into the next, especially when he is able to say, "Well done, my good and faithful servant." Imagine how great it will feel to hear those words from him! The Bible says in 1 Corinthians 2:9: "No eye has seen, no ear has heard, no mind has conceived what God has prepared for those who love him." It's unimaginable! Nothing in our common, every day experiences can possibly express how magnificent, how spectacular, how gorgeous, and how satisfying that new life will be.

Once in a while I have dreams where I write music so excruciatingly beautiful that tears stream down my cheeks, and I wake up tear-stained. As I dream I am surrounded by colors I have never seen before—or I'm in a mansion so gorgeous my jaw drops with amazement at the exquisiteness of the tapestries, the architecture, the art.

When I awaken from such dreams, I always feel as if God has allowed me a "glimpse through heaven's gate," to see, only for a moment, what lies in store for me. I never know when it will occur. I try to fall asleep again and recapture the glory, but I never can. It is a gift for that moment alone—a gift designed to give me hope, to continue my walk of faith, to keep on keeping on, until *finally* I see him face to face and he welcomes me into his kingdom—the one that has no end!

God will wipe every tear from their eyes. There will be no more death
or mourning or crying or pain, for the old order of things has passed away.

REVELATION 21:4

Our citizenship is in heaven.
And we eagerly await a Savior from there, the Lord Jesus Christ.

PHILIPPIANS 3:20

The Lamb at the center of the throne will be their shepherd;
he will lead them to springs of living water.
And God will wipe away every tear from their eyes.

REVELATION 7:17

The Lord himself will come down from heaven, with a loud command,
with the voice of the archangel and with the trumpet call of God,
and the dead in Christ will rise first. After that, we who are still alive and
are left will be caught up together with them in the clouds
to meet the Lord in the air. And so we will be with the Lord forever.

1 THESSALONIANS 4:16–17

Jesus said, "In my Father's house are many rooms; if it were not so, I would have told you. I am going there to prepare a place for you."

JOHN 14:2

Jesus said, "Rejoice that your names are written in heaven."

LUKE 10:20

Heavenly Father,

Thank you for giving me just a little glimpse, by faith, of the glory that is to come. I am amazed and grateful that you include me in your special plans. I offer you my giftedness, my hopes and dreams, my life. Whatever it costs me, wherever it leads me—I desire to fulfill the destiny you've planned for me. Amen.

Over a twenty-year period, I had the honor of interviewing most of
the "movers and shakers" of our culture—everyone from the
president of the United States to the latest soap star/sitcom star/hoops
star/movie star/hip-hop star/Broadway star. My job provided close-up and
personal encounters with many who live high-profile lifestyles at the top of
their game.

One of the things I noticed was that many of those people—most of them wealthy and considered wildly successful—seemed to be lost in the midst of their fame and fortune. They appeared certain of what they did (their jobs) and what they had (their possessions), but it was clear that they were quite uncertain of who they were.

Show business people really aren't so different from the rest of us. Their lives are often fraught with difficulties and obstacles similar to those encountered by builders, painters, electricians, plumbers, hairdressers, and those of every other profession. No matter what we do for a living, we all need the security of knowing that we are God's child. Riches often disappear, fame is fleeting, but a relationship with God never wavers in the storm or weakens with time.

The first time I clearly heard the good news of the gospel, I responded immediately and invited God into my heart and life. The simple message that God loved me and had a plan for me made perfect sense. Today, almost forty years later, I still cling tightly to God's hand. And I still find it difficult to understand why some people choose to exclude God from their lives—opting to go it alone in such a difficult, dangerous, uncaring world.

Do you have the assurance that you're a child of God? Is your identity securely anchored in him? If not, it can be. As you pursue excellence in your profession, be careful not to lose yourself in the process. Reach out until you *finally* find out who you are in him.

The Spirit himself testifies with our spirit

that we are God's children.

ROMANS 8:16

We are children of God, and what we will be has

not yet been made known. But we know that when he appears,

we shall be like him, for we shall see him as he is.

1 JOHN 3:2

How great is the love the Father has lavished on us,

that we should be called children of God. And that is what we are!

1 JOHN 3:1

Those who are lead by the Spirit of God are sons of God.

ROMANS 8:14

God sent the Spirit of his Son into our hearts,
the Spirit who calls out, "Abba, Father."

GALATIANS 4:6

Be imitators of God as dearly loved children and live a life of love,
just as Christ loved us and gave himself up
for us as a fragrant offering and sacrifice to God.

EPHESIANS 5:1–2

Heavenly Father,

My self esteem and security were all about doing more and having more. Now I know that has nothing to do with who I am. Help me to find myself in you and plant my roots in the rich soil of our relationship. Thank you for helping me to see myself as I really am—your imperfect but much-loved child. Amen.

HIS PASSION

I recently saw Mel Gibson's movie, "The Passion of the Christ" and was profoundly moved by it. The graphic depiction of the scourging and the crucifixion is something that has to be seen in all its horror to truly appreciate the magnitude of the sacrifice Jesus made for us.

In Mel's account, Jesus says, "It is accomplished" right before his spirit leaves his body. I had always read that he had said, "It is finished," but I loved Mel's translation because it meant not just Christ's suffering was over but his Mission—his whole purpose for being born—was accomplished. He had done what he set out to do, and in the process, he changed the world for all eternity.

Too often we have seen a cleaned-up version of Christ on the cross—a little blood on his forehead, his hands and his feet. But Scripture tells us that he was beaten so badly that he was unrecognizable as he hung dying on the cross. Forty lashes were known to kill a man, so the Romans administered 39 lashes. Yet Jesus was still able to carry the cross almost all the way to Golgotha.

I have been to Israel three times, and I know how challenging the terrain is. Jesus had been a carpenter by trade. Using the carpentry tools of the day would have required him to be fit. In addition, Jesus traveled by foot for three years, preaching all over the country. Scripture mentions he traveled by boat occasionally and by donkey as he entered Jerusalem five days before his crucifixion. But usually he traveled on foot.

This was hardly the "wimpy" Jesus we have seen portrayed in art and movies. Such a person would not have survived the scourging, much less a significant time on the cross. At one point in the movie, my daughter Cassidy leaned over to me and said, "Mommy, the beating lasted too long." It certainly did. But that's what made the movie so powerful—it didn't downplay the suffering.

Man's inhumanity to man has always been difficult for me to watch. But man's inhumanity to God was close to unbearable. Near the end as I was sobbing, Cassidy whispered, "Don't cry, Mommy. It has a happy ending. Remember?" Just the same, I kept my eyes open and focused until the last frame of the film. I didn't want to miss a moment of the truth.

It was our weaknesses Christ carried; it was our sorrows that weighed
him down. And we thought his troubles were a punishment from God
for his own sins! But he was wounded and crushed for our sins. He was
beaten that we might have peace. He was whipped, and we were healed!
All of us have strayed away like sheep. We have left God's paths to follow
our own. Yet the LORD laid on him the guilt and sins of us all.

He was oppressed and treated harshly, yet he never said a word. He was
led as a lamb to the slaughter. And as a sheep is silent before the
shearers, he did not open his mouth. From prison and trial they led him
away to his death. But who among the people realized that he was dying
for their sins—that he was suffering their punishment? He had done no
wrong, and he never deceived anyone. But he was buried like a
criminal; he was put in a rich man's grave.

But it was the LORD's good plan to crush him and fill him with grief.
Yet when his life is made an offering for sin, he will have a multitude of
children, many heirs. He will enjoy a long life, and the LORD's plan will

prosper in his hands. When he sees all that is accomplished by his anguish, he will be satisfied. And because of what he has experienced, my righteous servant will make it possible for many to be counted righteous, for he will bear all their sins.

ISAIAH 53:4–11 NLT

Lamb of God,

What amazes me most was your silence. "You were led as a lamb to the slaughter, and as a sheep before its shearers is silent, you opened not your mouth." The silence of the lamb. Why? You knew you were in the hands of God. You knew your death would redeem your people. You knew you would glorify God. You knew you would fulfill your destiny. You knew you wouldn't stay dead. Jesus, that's why I'm sticking with you. Amen.

OUR LOVING
Eyes

Our Loving Eyes

Kathie Lee Gifford/Phil Sillas

We looked at one another so many years ago
And found something special in our eyes
We vowed to each other that
There would never be another
For if love is truly real, it never dies

Now here we are
Weathered by the years
Strengthened by the trials
Tethered by the tears

No need to speak of all that we share
It comes as no surprise
That we'll continue our sweet romance
With our eyes, our loving eyes

No need to speak of all that we feel
We know what's true, We know what's real
And until we whisper the last of our last goodbyes
We'll continue our romance
With our loving eyes

We've dreamed our dreams together,
We've walked the narrow road
We've shared every burden side by side
And as we turned each corner
We turned to God above
Depending on his grace to sanctify our love

Now we sit by the fire
Weathered by the years
Strengthened by the trials
Tendered by the tears

TRUE *Love*

Many of my family members were introduced to the gospel for the first time through the ministry of Dr. Billy Graham, and we continue to be inspired by his extraordinary commitment to share the hope that is ours as believers.

Recently a friend returned from a ministry seminar in Montreat, North Carolina—Billy and Ruth Graham's home. While he was there, he asked Billy how Ruth was feeling, knowing that she has had many health problems in recent years.

Billy smiled that wonderful "Billy" smile and answered, "Ruth is doing just fine. She's in a wheelchair now and can't get around too well." Billy's eyes began to twinkle. "So we continue our romance with our eyes."

I cried when my friend recounted the story, thinking of those two incredible ambassadors of God who have served the Lord and each other so faithfully for so many years. Knowing they had just celebrated their sixtieth wedding anniversary, I asked the Lord to help me write a song that would honor their love.

When I read the lyrics to my Mother, she began to cry. "Oh honey, it's a beautiful song. Your daddy and I loved each other in the same way." She was right. Like the Grahams, my mom and dad had shared a special relationship until my father passed away after a long illness. Toward the end of his life, my daddy could no longer walk, feed himself, or even speak. But his eyes would follow my mother's every movement as she went about the room, caring for him.

In a culture where we fixate on romantic/sexual love, it is rare to see a celebration of true and lasting love like that shared by couples like Billy and Ruth Graham and my parents. Way too often, couples give up on each other when romantic feelings wane and hard times touch their lives. They never discover the tremendous blessing gained by seeing a marriage commitment through to the end.

Don't get me wrong. I realize that it takes great fortitude and strength of character to weather the storms of life together. But as couples like the Grahams and my parents can tell you, the reward for a lifelong commitment is a love much deeper than newlyweds could imagine—a love that transcends the physical and reaches into the soul.

It's time to honor couples that trust God until the moment when they whisper their last goodbyes—through loving eyes.

A man will leave his father and mother
and be united to his wife, and they will become one flesh.

Jesus said, "'The two will become one flesh.'
So they are no longer two, but one.
Therefore what God has joined together, let man not separate."

There is no fear in love. But perfect love drives out fear.

Many waters cannot quench love;
rivers cannot wash it away.

The eyes of the LORD range throughout the earth

to strengthen those whose hearts are fully committed to him.

2 CHRONICLES 16:9

My eyes are fixed on you, O Sovereign LORD;

in you I take refuge.

PSALM 141:8

O God,

You are the brilliant creator of marriage and family. I ask you to transform my heart, renew my mind, and free me to see my spouse with new eyes—the eyes of love. I re-dedicate my marriage to you, Lord. From this moment on, I ask you to teach us to live together as friends, partners, and lovers. Amen.

WE CAN DEPEND
ON HIS WORD.
Reprise

WE CAN DEPEND ON HIS WORD
—REPRISE

Kathie Lee Gifford, Phil Sillas

When my life is over
And the battle is done
I have his assurance
That the battle was won
And life everlasting is waiting for me
He's made a pathway through the clouds
Through the storm
Through the desert
Through the darkness
Through the sea

He's made a pathway through the clouds
To all eternity
For you and me

He's the Alpha Omega
The beginning and the end
And we can depend on his word
We can depend on his word

THE BASIS
of My Trust

Have you ever been disappointed? Have you been disappointed so many times that you have trouble believing anybody's promises are for real? You're not alone. We've all been burned. We've all been disappointed, and we've all done our fair share of disappointing others. That's why God's promises are so powerful—he never breaks them!

I realized recently that I have good health. I have friends. I have family. And I have financial stability. The problem is that I really can't count on any of them. All I can count on is the word of the Lord Jesus, who said: "The words I have spoken to you are spirit and they are life" (John 6:63). My health could be gone in an instant, friends and family are human beings who oftentimes disappoint us, and financial fortunes come and go. The only one worthy of my unqualified trust is Jesus.

Jesus didn't just say that we can depend on him—he proved it by sacrificing his own pure body on a Roman cross. He walked the walk! All the way along the Via Della Rosa. All the way to the Place of the Skull— the town dump. He couldn't have chosen a fouler, more putrid place to lay down his life than the cesspool that was Golgotha. All the garbage from Jerusalem was taken there to be disposed of—to be forgotten.

And if Jesus had merely been a man, he would have been forgotten there too—just another statistic. Just another useless rabble-rouser during the tempestuous years of Roman reign in Palestine. But Jesus wasn't just a man. He was the instrument of God's plan to redeem mankind from their sin and allow them to sit at the banquet table of eternity beside their Savior who made it all possible.

It's so magnificent a plan and so outrageous a cost that my heart and soul can barely contain the enormity of it. But I can and I will *depend* on it!

*It is better to take refuge in the L*ORD
     than to trust in man.
*It is better to take refuge in the L*ORD
     than to trust in princes.

PSALM 118:8–9

Some trust in chariots and some in horses,
     *but we trust in the name of the L*ORD *our God.*
They are brought to their knees and fall,
     but we rise up and stand firm.

PSALM 20:7–8

*This is what the Sovereign L*ORD *says:*
     "See, I lay a stone in Zion,
          a tested stone,
     a precious cornerstone for a sure foundation;
          the one who trusts will never be dismayed."

ISAIAH 28:16

Blessed is the man who trusts in the LORD,

   whose confidence is in him.

JEREMIAH 17:7

Blessed is the man

   who makes the LORD *his trust.*

PSALM 40:4

Trust in the LORD *forever,*

   for the LORD, *the* LORD, *is the Rock eternal.*

ISAIAH 26:4

Mighty God,

Trust is a precious commodity. And a high-risk venture. In my life I have sometimes betrayed trust, abused trust, and misplaced trust—anchoring my hope in all the wrong people and all the wrong gods. And I have paid dearly for it. You could have written me off. You would have been justified. But instead, you dragged yourself to Calvary, to Golgotha, to the place of the skull. And there "you endured the cross, and despised the shame"—and earned my trust forever. Amen.